S0-BAT-249

Nature's Children

SNAKES

Merebeth Switzer
and
Katherine Grier

 Grolier

FACTS IN BRIEF

Classification of North American snakes
   Class: *Reptilia* (reptiles)
   Order: *Ophidia* (snakes)
   Family: North America has five families of snakes.
   Genus: There are fifty genera of snakes in North America.
   Species: Approximately 320 species and subspecies of snakes are found in North America.

World distribution.   Varies with species.

Habitat.   Varies with species.

Distinctive physical characteristics.   Long slim limbless body covered with dry scales; no external ears.

Habits.   Vary with species.

Diet.   All species are meat-eaters.

Published originally as
"Getting to Know . . . Nature's Children."

This series is approved and recommended by the Federation of Ontario Naturalists.

This library reinforced edition is available exclusively from:

Grolier Educational Corporation
Sherman Turnpike, Danbury, Connecticut 06816

Contents

When you see a snake gliding through the grass or basking on a warm rock, what do you feel?

People often feel strongly about snakes. In many stories, snakes are portrayed as villains. But different kinds of stories have also been told.

Long ago the Greek people saw that snakes shed their old worn skins to reveal a fine new skin beneath. They thought of this new skin as a sign of life and health. Doctors today still use a picture of two snakes curling up a staff as the sign of their profession.

One thing is certain. Snakes have been misunderstood. What are snakes really like? Only careful watching can tell. You can begin yourself. And naturalists who study snakes can tell us much more about how they live and how they are suited for the role they play in the natural world.

Scaly Relatives

Snakes are reptiles. So are lizards, turtles, alligators and crocodiles. That means that they are covered with tough, dry scales rather than fur or feathers. Their young usually hatch from eggs. They breathe air into lungs. And, unlike people, they have no built-in temperature control. Their temperature is affected by the temperature of the air, water or earth around them. In these ways, all reptiles are the same.

But in other ways snakes are different from their reptile relatives. How? One big difference is easy to see. Snakes do not have legs. A few still have small bones and a claw left where their ancestors had hip and leg bones, but these leg leftovers do not help the snake move.

Why don't snakes have legs? Scientists think that long ago, snakes' lizard-like ancestors began to hunt for food in other animals' burrows. But their legs got in the way in such narrow spaces. Very gradually their legs disappeared so that snakes could hunt more successfully underground.

Opposite page:

The Northern Red-bellied Snake is usually active at night.

Snakes, Snakes and More Snakes

About 320 different kinds of snakes live in North America. They need food, water, warmth and shelter to live. They find these in many different kinds of places. Some snakes live in deserts while others live in forests, grasslands or mountains. Some spend much of their time burrowing underground, and others live almost entirely above ground. There are snakes almost everywhere in North America and the rest of the world, except in the far north where the winters are very long and cold. There are no snakes in Iceland, Ireland and New Zealand.

The beautiful Smooth Green Snake is rarely seen because it blends in so well with the surrounding greenery.

Long and Slim

Some snakes are huge. The largest snakes in the world can grow as long as five men lying head to toe. But in North America, the largest snakes only grow as long as a man is tall. The shortest is about the length of a new pencil. Most are somewhere in between.

Big or small, a snake's basic shape is the same—long and slim. The snake has many organs that are almost the same as yours, doing the same sorts of jobs: breathing in air, pumping and cleaning the blood, taking the nourishment from food and getting rid of what is left.

But how do all those organs fit? They become long and slim just like the snake's body. And if there were once two organs of one kind, one has shrunk or disappeared completely.

Occasionally snakes are born all black instead of their regular color. This Garter Snake is hard to recognize without its stripes.

A Skin of Scales

A snake's skin is made up of many scales. There are small scales on its back and sides and larger ones on its head. Running from head to tail along its belly is a row of big rectangular scales called scutes.

A snake's scales look like separate pieces of skin, but they are not. The snake's outer skin is all one piece. In between the scales, there are hidden folds of skin that join each scale to the next one. These folds let the skin stretch as the snake curves its body or swallows a large meal.

A snake has three layers of skin. The inner one holds the snake's colors and patterns. The middle one is like a factory, always building the outer layer. The outer layer is transparent and hard and thin. It is made of the same substance as your fingernails and protects the snake from rough objects as its moves along the ground. This outer skin even covers the snake's eyes, like a clear bubble. In fact, the eyes are protected by this layer of skin instead of by eyelids that close. That is why a snake's eyes are always open, even when it is asleep.

Opposite page:

You can tell the Garter Snake is active during the day by its round pupils. Snakes that move at night have slit-like pupils similar to a cat's.

Changing Skins

You lose tiny flakes of old skin every day, but a snake sheds its old outer skin all in one piece. Shedding its skin is important for a snake.

Young snakes need room for their growing bodies, but their outer skins never grow. So they must grow new, larger ones, usually about six times a year. Older snakes do not grow as fast, but their skins get worn with use. They shed a few times a year.

A snake's old skin must separate from the new one before it can be shed. A milky liquid builds up under the outer skin and loosens it. It even covers the snake's eyes so that it cannot see very well. A few days later the snake rubs its nose against a twig and makes a break in the old skin. Then it slithers out of it, peeling it off inside out as you would pull a sweater over your head.

The old skin is clear but it shows the outline of every scale and the folds of skin in between. The new skin is fresh and shiny, and the snake's colors and patterns show up more brightly than ever through it.

Garter Snake shedding its skin.

Opposite page:

An Eastern Milk Snake about to shed. Note the foggy eye.

No Arms, No Legs—But Can They Move

Think for a moment of the parts of your body you use when you walk, run or swim. It is hard to imagine moving without arms and legs, isn't it? But a snake does not have arms or legs—or fins or wings. How, then, can it move so easily and gracefully?

The snake has a backbone that runs from the base of its head to the tip of its tail. This backbone is made up of many small bones that are all connected. Each one can move slightly sideways and up and down. These bones let the snake curve back and forth.

But a snake's bones could not go anywhere without the muscles that are attached to them. A snake moves by tightening or relaxing its muscles, just as you do. The muscles pull or push the bones so that the snake's whole body moves forward. To help move itself along, the snake grabs on to twigs or rocks or bark with its belly scales. They give the snake its grip and keep it from slipping backwards.

Opposite page:

Coiled and ready to strike. (Pacific Rattlesnake)

Different Places, Different Moves

Just as you can, a snake can move in several different ways. It can wriggle forward, curving its body into an S. In water or on land, this is the way most snakes travel.

Or a snake can side-wind. The snake curves its body into loops and throws each loop sideways, clear of the ground. Snakes use side-winding in shifting sand where scutes cannot get a good grip. And because only the bends of each loop touch the ground, many snakes side-wind if they are moving across hot sand.

A snake can also push and pull itself up trees or along narrow passages. First it curves the front half of its body into tight loops and grips with its front scutes. Next, it pulls the back half of its body forward into new loops and takes hold with its rear scutes. Then it begins all over again.

Milk Snake.

Finally, a snake can creep along in an almost straight line. For a long, heavy snake this is much easier than weaving from side to side. Its muscles lift and pull a scute ahead. The scute grips the ground where it lands. Then the muscles move the next scute ahead and the next and the next. The muscles pull the snake's body forward bit by bit.

Most snakes have one favorite way of traveling, such as side-winding. But many use a combination of moves. For example, a heavy snake that usually creeps forward in a straight line can use the wavy S if it needs to move fast.

You might think that snakes move easily only on land, but most snakes can also swim if they have to. Some water snakes even hunt for food in the shallows of lakes and rivers and swim long distances across open water.

Even though a water snake spends a great deal of time searching for food in ponds and lakes, it sleeps on dry ground.

Snake Sense

You learn about your world by seeing, hearing, touching, smelling and tasting it. Snakes learn about their world a little differently.

Using its heat sensors, a viper and some other snakes can hunt and strike in total darkness.

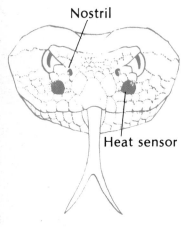

Nostril

Heat sensor

Snakes' eyes and ears do not work the way yours do. They cannot see very clearly or tell how far away things are. And snakes do not have ears like yours with eardrums that pick up sounds carried by air. So when a snake charmer plays a flute, the snake does not hear a sound. It sways to the charmer's movements, not his music.

But a snake's eyes can spot tiny movements. And it has inner ears that pick up vibrations from the ground.

A snake's sense of touch is more like yours. Although its skin is scaly, it can feel all over. And many snakes that prey on warm-blooded animals have special heat sensors that tell them if something warm—and maybe good to eat— is nearby.

Sidewinder.

A Tongue with a Difference

Although a snake learns a lot about its world
through vibration and touch, it learns most
by using its tongue. A snake's tongue is
long and forked at the end. It can hardly
taste things at all, but it *can* smell
things. How?

If you watch a snake you will see that it is
always darting its tongue in and out of its
mouth. The tongue picks up tiny bits of scent
information from the air and the ground.
When the snake pulls its tongue back into its
mouth, it puts the forked tips into two small
holes in the roof of its mouth. These holes
work just like your nose. They send signals to
the snake's brain to tell it what it has
''smelled'' with its tongue.

Garter Snake.

Skilled Hunters

All snakes, big and small, are meat-eaters. But they catch their prey in different ways. Some catch and hold their prey with their teeth before eating it live. Some are constrictors. They coil around their prey and squeeze it so it cannot breathe. And others poison their catch by spurting venom into it through long, hollow fangs. The venom is made in a small venom gland at the back of the mouth.

Once a snake has caught its prey, it eats it whole. It cannot do anything else. It does not have sharp cutting teeth or flat chewing teeth. Its teeth are pointy and curved inward and good for holding onto its prey.

Depending on its size, a snake eats insects, frogs, mice, rats, other snakes, larger animals or the remains of other hunters' kills. Often a snake eats a meal several times bigger than its mouth.

These fangs will swing outward when the snake attacks and pull back into their sheaths when the snake closes its mouth.

Sheath

Fang

This Pacific Rattlesnake has taken over a magpie nest.

Super Swallowers

Imagine trying to swallow an apple whole. Could you do it? Of course you couldn't. So how can a snake swallow something larger than its own head? To a snake, big mouthfuls are not a problem. Its jaw bones can separate from the rest of its skull and from each other to stretch open. The bottom jaw bones even split in the middle. Now the snake has a huge mouth and no bones to get in the way.

But even with such a big mouth, swallowing is a slow business. Bit by bit, the snake works its jaws around its prey. Soon its throat starts to tighten and pulls the animal into the snake's stomach. Before long there is no sign of the prey—except for a bulge moving slowly down the snake's body.

A snake that has swallowed a big meal may take days or even weeks to digest all of it. During that time it will not need to eat anything else.

As its name suggests, the Blue Racer can move very quickly when it wants to.

Avoiding Danger

Snakes have many enemies in the natural world—meat-eating birds and animals, some reptiles and even other snakes.

Some snakes have colors and patterns that help them hide from their enemies. For example, it is difficult to see a green snake among leaves or grass, or a mottled black and brown snake among rocks or sand. Other snakes are brightly colored. Many of them are very poisonous. Some people think that their bright colors warn their enemies that they are dangerous.

When a snake senses danger, the first thing it does is try to get away. If it cannot flee, it tries to protect itself.

The Southern Ring-necked Snake is also known as the "corkscrew" snake.

30

Defense Tactics

Some kinds of snakes try to scare their enemies away. They hiss or rattle their tails or puff themselves up so they look big and ferocious. Others give off a smelly, terrible-tasting musk if they are picked up. And some even roll over and pretend to be dead.

A few snakes are quick to attack. But most strike only if they cannot escape or scare off their enemies. The weapons they use to defend themselves are the same ones they use for hunting. Some bite, some use venom and some try to squeeze their enemies so they cannot breathe.

A rattlesnake's tail has several horny rings that rattle against each other when the snake shakes it. The sound is a warning not to be ignored: "Back off or else!" (Western Diamond Rattlesnake)

33

Too Hot? Too Cold?

You are warm-blooded. This means your body automatically controls its own temperature so it stays much the same no matter how hot or cold the weather is.

Snakes are cold-blooded. Their bodies do not control their temperature as ours do. If it gets cold out, the snake's temperature drops. If it gets hot, so does the snake. But snakes like the same range of temperature we do— T-shirt weather. That is when their bodies work best and they are alert and agile.

Snakes must control their temperature by moving to places where it is warmer or cooler. A snake warms itself by basking in the sun out of the wind. It can cool itself by seeking shade or wet shorelines or by going undergound.

Big snakes do not live in cool climates. It would be too hard for them to keep warm. Many snakes that do live where it is cooler are brown or black. Their dark colors take in the sun's warmth much faster than lighter colors and help them keep warm.

Opposite page:

Small Brown or De Kay Snake

Overleaf:

The Hog-nosed Snake is a great bluffer. When threatened it spreads its neck like a Cobra, opens its mouth and hisses, but it has never been known to bite.

Away from Winter's Chill

How do snakes in cold-weather country survive winter? As the days grow shorter and colder, snakes move more and more slowly and become less and less alert. When it is too chilly for them to warm themselves by lying in the sun, they must look for shelter. They need protection from freezing weather and from alert, warm-blooded enemies.

A snake's winter shelter is called the snake's hibernaculum. A crevice in rocks, a space beneath a log or an animal's underground burrow will all serve as a hibernaculum.

Once it has found shelter, the snake hibernates for the whole winter. Its heart beats more slowly. It breathes less often. And because it stays still, it uses so little energy that it does not need to eat again until spring.

Some snakes hibernate alone, but a large pit or burrow can attract many snakes. Different kinds of snakes and sometimes even enemies will pass the winter side by side. Once a snake has found a shelter, it will return to the same place year after year.

Opposite page:

Cluster of rattlesnakes.

Spring Mating

As the spring days grow warmer and longer, snakes that have spent the winter hibernating wriggle out of their shelters. The warm weather tells them that now is the time to mate. The male finds the female by following the scent she leaves on the ground. Snakes often mate with different partners during mating season.

Sometimes two males pretend to fight to decide which one will mate with a female. They lift their heads, twist their bodies together and try to upset each other's balance. But they do not bite or hiss. Eventually the weaker snake leaves.

The Kingsnake is truly the king of snakes. It can attack even poisonous rattlesnakes since it is not harmed by their venom.

A New Year, New Babies

Baby snakes start their lives in different ways. Their mother may look for a warm, safe place to lay eggs—perhaps in a rotting log, a burrow or under leaves. Some kinds of snakes lay as few as 7 eggs while others lay as many as 60.

The eggs are white but are not brittle like chicken eggs. Instead, they feel like ping-pong balls, only a little softer. Inside the egg, the baby snake feeds on the yolk. When it is ready to hatch, it uses a small, sharp egg-tooth to chip its way through the shell. Soon after its work is done, the egg-tooth drops off.

Eastern Hog-nosed Snake hatching.

Other baby snakes live inside eggs which their mother carries inside her until they are ready to hatch. These babies also live on their egg's yolk. But the shells of their eggs are thin. They break open as they are pushed from the mother's body.

A few kinds of baby snakes are born live. They live inside a clear sac inside their mother's body. When they are born, their first job is to break out of their sac.

Young Eastern Milk Snake.

A Hard Start

Life is dangerous for a baby snake. Its mother leaves as soon as the eggs are laid or the babies are born. Many eggs and babies become food for other hunters, but many survive.

Baby snakes are like their parents in every way but size. For their first few years, they grow quickly. In places where the weather stays warm, young snakes grow all year. Snakes that hibernate do not grow during the winter, but they grow extra fast once the warm weather returns. In fact, snakes never really stop growing, although older snakes grow so slowly that you would hardly notice it.

Naturalists do not know how long snakes live in the wild. But they can guess because they have watched snakes in captivity. There, large snakes often live for more than twenty years and smaller ones often live to be ten or fifteen.

Words to Know

Egg tooth A hard point on the tip of a baby snake's nose which it uses to break its way out of its shell.

Fangs Long sharp hollow teeth through which venom flows in some snakes.

Heat sensors Organs that are specially sensitive to temperature.

Hibernaculum The place where a snake or group of snakes hibernates.

Hibernate To go into a deep sleep for the entire winter.

Mating season The time of year during which animals come together to produce young.

Musk A strong smelling substance produced by some animals.

Organs Parts of the body adapted for a particular vital function.

Prey An animal hunted by another animal for food.

Scales Thin, hard overlapping plates that protect a snake's skin.

Scutes The big rectangular scales on a snake's belly.

Venom Poisonous fluid produced by some snakes.

INDEX

Cover Photo: Brian Milne (First Light Associated Photographers)
Photo Credits: Norman Lightfoot (Eco-Art Productions), pages 4, 11, 20, 37, 41;
Bill Ivy, pages 7, 8, 12, 15, 19, 24, 31, 34, 45; Tom W. Hall (Miller Services),
pages 16, 28; Robert C. Simpson (Valan Photos), pages 23, 42; Dennis Schmidt
(Valan Photos), page 27; E. Degginger (Miller Services), page 32; Gerhard
Kahrmann (Valan Photos), page 38.

Printed and Bound in Italy by Lego Sp